CONTENTS

KU-070-804

INTRODUCTION

Hockey, known as field hockey in Canada and the USA, is a fast, skilful sport governed by the Fédération Internationale de Hockey (FIH). Although it is claimed that hockey has origins as far back as 2000BC, the modern game is thought to have originated from around 1750–1850.

Ben Hawes of Great Britain and England.

THE GAME

Hockey is played by two teams, each consisting of 11 players on the field. It is strongly recommended that there are ten outfield players and one properly equipped goalkeeper (see page 9). However, the FIH rules permit the use of 11 field players. Schools are strongly advised always to play with a goalkeeper. Each team must have a captain who wears an armband so that he or she can be recognised. The captain is responsible for the conduct of his or her team.

The captains toss a coin to determine either possession of the ball to start the game or which end to defend. Teams change ends after half-time. The team that did not have possession to start the game has possession to start the second half.

Each team defends its own half of the field and attacks the other. The aim of the game is to score goals by the attacking team playing the ball with the stick into the goal. The ball must be struck by the attacking team from inside a limited area known as the striking circle. An own goal can be scored from an attacker striking in the circle, and the ball deflecting into goal from a defending player.

There is a variety of systems of play that are used in hockey. For example, 5-3-2, 4-4-2, 4-3-3 and 3-3-1-3 (see page 33). Other variations exist, but these are the main systems played.

Other forms of hockey include indoor hockey, which is a very fast moving, exciting and skilful game. England Hockey also promotes zone hockey (see page 57), which is where disabled and able-bodied players can play together.

SUBSTITUTIONS

A team may have as many as 16 players, with the five players not on the pitch able to be used as substitutes. They can be brought on to the field at any time except when a penalty corner (see page 46) is awarded or is under way. All substitutions on and off the field take place at the halfway line. The team captains are responsible for ensuring that substitution is carried out correctly, although in some games, team officials, usually the manager or the coach, handle this.

A defending goalkeeper who is injured or suspended when a penalty corner is awarded or being taken may be substituted.

After a competitive international match in the 2006 Commonwealth Games, English and Australian players display good sportsmanship by shaking hands.

THE RULES OF HOCKEY

The complete *Rules of Hockey* is published every year by the Hockey Rules Board and can be obtained from England Hockey at its website: www.englandhockey.co.uk or from the FIH at their website: www.fihockey.org.

THE PITCH

The best pitch is an artificial turf with either a sand, sand-dressed or water base. Artificial pitch numbers are increasing and offer a true surface which inexperienced players find easier to play on and enjoy. Almost all league games are played on artificial turf.

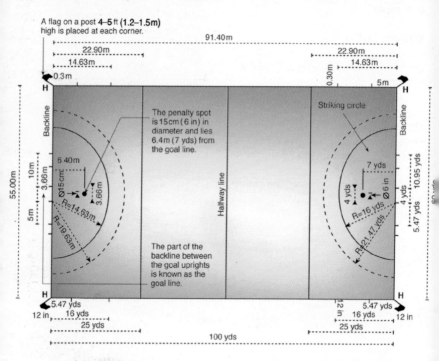

A flag on a post **4–5** ft (1.2–1.5m) high is placed at each corner.

91.40m

22.90m

14.63m

0.3m

0.30m

5m

H — Backline

The penalty spot is 15cm (6 in) in diameter and lies 6.4m (7 yds) from the goal line.

Striking circle

Backline — H

6.40m

3.66m

Ø15cm

3.66m

R=14.63m

R=19.63m

The part of the backline between the goal uprights is known as the goal line.

Halfway line

7 yds

4 yds

Ø 6 in

4 yds

R=16 yds

R=21.47 yds

10m

5m

55.00m

10.95 yds

5.47 yds

H

5.47 yds

12 in 16 yds

25 yds

12 in

5.47 yds

16 yds

25 yds

12 in

100 yds

THE GOAL AND STRIKING CIRCLE

The goal is placed at the centre of the outer edge of the backline. It is rectangular, painted white and has a net fitted to its upright posts and

crossbar. The net is fitted to back and side boards at least 46cm (18 in) high. The side boards make the goal at least 1.2m (4 ft) deep. The striking or shooting circle is a D-shaped area, marked out in front of each goal with a radius of 14.63m

(16 yds) from each goal post. A dotted or broken line is marked 5m (5½ yds) outside and running parallel with the striking circle.

THE PENALTY SPOT

In front of each goal is a spot, known as the penalty spot. It is 15cm (6 in) in diameter and 6.4m (7 yds) in front of the inner edge of the goal line.

OTHER LINES

On 'old' pitches, short lines 30cm (1 ft) long are marked on the backline at 5- and 10-m (5.5- and 11-yd) intervals from the goalposts. On newer, metric, pitches, 30-cm (1-ft) lines are marked 5 and 10m (5.5 and 11 yds) from the goalposts. Similar lines are marked on the sidelines 5m (5½ yds) from the corner flags and on the sideline in line with the top of the circle.

RESPONSIBILITY FOR CONDITION

In club games, the captain of the home or host team is responsible for the pitch, flags, goals and goal nets being safe and in good condition, as well as ensuring spectators can be controlled. At higher levels, match officials perform these tasks.

The goal is 3.66m (12 ft) wide by 2.14m (7 ft) high on the inside measurements of the posts. The uprights and crossbar are 51mm (2 in) wide by 75mm (3 in) deep.

A hockey pitch is 91.4m (100 yds) long by 55m (60 yds) wide and is split across its width into four 23-m (25-yd) quarters by continuous lines.

EQUIPMENT

The individual equipment needed for players, with the exception of goalkeepers, is relatively minimal. It does need to be in good condition, within the rules and safe.

THE STICK

The stick is made of wood or any material containing wood, but must not contain metal. Many modern players now use composite material sticks. Sticks are normally straight or largely straight from the top of the handle to the beginning of the crooked or hooked lower end. The hooked stick head has a flat side on the left of the hook. That flat side and the part of the stick above it, together with its edges, are the parts of the stick which can play the ball. Players are not allowed to play the ball with the back of the stick. 'Left-handed' sticks do not exist. However, the left hand controls the stick movement.

Sticks can wear so umpires will check that sticks are safe, especially assessing splintered or chipped stick heads. The use of tapes and resins to repair the sticks is allowed provided the stick does not exceed maximum circumference.

BALL

The ball is round, hard and similar in size and weight to a cricket ball. A dimpled ball is used on synthetic pitches. It may be made of any material and is usually covered in plastic. It can be coloured white or any other suitable colour, although colour-blind players and umpires normally prefer using a white ball. The rules of hockey specify the ball's precise weight and dimensions.

Richard Alexander (England) accelerating away from his opponents, South Africa, in the 2006 World Cup.

UNIFORM

Players are required to dress in their team's colours, with the shorts and socks worn by one team being a different colour to their opponents' clothing. Women generally play in skirts, but more lately in skorts (skirt with cycling shorts combined). Competitive hockey usually requires players to have clear numbers on the backs of their shirts. Players keep the same number if the match requires them to change their shirt colour. Players may not wear jewellery or baseball caps/hats with sharp peaks that might injure others.

GOALKEEPER'S EQUIPMENT

Goalkeepers must wear a full helmet and a shirt with numbers on both the front and back. The helmet must be worn throughout the game, although it is sometimes allowed to be taken off when taking (but not defending) a penalty stroke. The shirt must be a different colour to those worn by both their own side and the opposing team. Goalkeepers usually wear protective footwear called kickers as well as leg guards, thigh and chest padding and gloves or hand protectors. It is highly recommended that goalkeepers also wear a box, pelvic protector and a throat guard.

THE UMPIRES

See page 54 for information on the umpires and their equipment.

A goalkeeper in full protective clothing concentrates on the game.

Shinguards and mouth guards are highly recommended to be worn by all players.

PLAYING THE GAME

A full game of hockey is made up of two 35-minute periods separated by a 5–10 minute-long half-time period. There are specific ways of starting each half of the game and restarting the game after goals or stoppages.

EXTRA TIME

In some competitions, a game drawn at full-time may require extra time to be played. This normally starts after a 5-minute break and is made up of two 7-minute periods separated by a 3-minute interval. The captains toss a coin before the first extra time period to determine end and possession in a similar way to starting the match.

TO START A HALF AND RESTART AFTER A GOAL

The first half is started by a player of the team that did not choose ends. After half-time a player from the opposing side restarts the game. After a goal, the game is restarted by the team scored against and the umpire who awarded the goal. Teams must be in their own half of the pitch. When the umpire blows the whistle, the ball may be pushed or hit in any direction.

GOLDEN GOALS AND SHOOTOUTS

Some competitions use a golden goal rule in extra time with the first goal determining the winner. If no goal is scored, the game usually goes into a penalty stroke competition (see *Rules of Hockey*).

▶ England's Kate Walsh with the New Zealand captain, with both umpires looking on prior to starting the game.

GENERAL RULE

A general series of rules apply whenever a team is awarded sole or exclusive possession of the ball to:

- start each half
- put the ball into play
- take a free hit
- take a penalty corner.

Whenever a team is in one of the above situations, the opposing team must retreat and be at least 5m (5½ yds) away from the player playing the ball. The following actions must also occur:

- the ball must be stationary
- the ball must be pushed or hit
- the ball must not be raised intentionally from the ground or played dangerously

- the player playing the ball must move the ball at least 1m (3 ft) before any team-mate can play it.

After taking the stroke, the player may not approach or remain within playing distance of the ball until another player of either side has played it.

Remember that the clock is not stopped when a goal is awarded. This can be important when a game nears its end.

An England player accelerates away, eliminating two New Zealand players.

OPEN PLAY

In open play, players may hit, flick, aerial or push the ball safely in any direction. They must use the flat 'front' of their stick head or the flat area above it to play the ball. Players may raise the ball to any height, provided they do not directly endanger other players or cause them to play dangerously – for example, by raising their sticks above their shoulders to play an aerial ball.

▼ A tackling player (in yellow) stretches to try to jab the ball out of the control of his opponent.

Physical contact

Hockey is essentially a non-contact sport. Players may tackle for the ball generally from the front or side-on with their sticks, but may not intentionally make physical contact with each other. Nor may they make deliberate physical contact with each other's sticks. Hockey, though, is an extremely fast-moving game and, as a result, some physical contact is inevitable. Umpires check to ensure that the ball is played properly before any other contact between players or their sticks is made.

Shielding the ball

The player may shield the ball to maintain possession, but must keep his or her feet moving at all times away from the opposition (a player with the ball must not back into his or her opponent). It prevents players from shielding the ball with their sticks or their bodies when they are being tackled. Both the player in possession of the ball and the potential tackler have a duty of care and must play within the rules of the game.

Tackling

When tackling, a player must:

- be in the right position

- display intent to play the ball, i.e. with the stick on or near the ground

- use proper timing when approaching the ball with the stick.

The England women's team celebrate after winning the bronze medal in the 2006 Commonwealth Games.

INTENTIONAL CONTACT

Umpires look out for intentional physical contact such as pushing, pulling, barging or hitting of sticks. These actions are considered detrimental to the game. If intentional physical contact is made, it is normally penalised with both a match penalty and a personal penalty (see page 50).

BALL OUT OF PLAY

The ball may be sent out of play over the sideline or the backline by either team. If the ball goes out over the sideline, it, or another ball, is placed on the line where it left the pitch. A player of the team that did not put the ball out of play may hit or push it according to the rules on pages 10–11.

OVER THE BACKLINE

If the ball is sent out of play over the backline, one of three decisions result depending on who takes the ball over.

1. Taken out by an attacker

The ball is placed on the ground opposite to where it went over the backline and up to 14.63m (16 yds) up the pitch from the backline. A defender then hits or pushes the ball into play.

2. Taken out unintentionally by a defender

The ball is placed on the corner mark on the sideline on whichever side of the goal the ball left the pitch. It is then hit or pushed into play by a player of the attacking side.

3. Taken out intentionally by a defender

A goal can be scored if the ball was struck by an attacker inside the striking circle and the defender takes the ball over the goal line. If no goal is scored, then a penalty corner is awarded against the defending team.

INTENTIONAL OR NOT?

Umpires need to be particularly careful when deciding whether a ball is sent out of play intentionally by defenders, especially by goalkeepers. As a general guide, if a goalkeeper uses the foot nearest the backline to clear the ball and it goes out of play, it may be unintentional. If the foot furthest from the backline is used, there may be intent.

A player scores a reverse-stick goal.

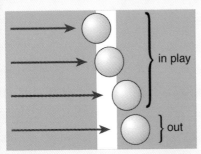

For the ball to go out of play, it needs to completely cross the line.

England's Simon Mantell takes a shot at India's goal in the 2006 Word Cup – England beat India 3-2.

SCORING A GOAL

For a goal to be scored in open play, the ball must be played by an attacker within the striking circle and pass completely over the goal line. It does not matter if the ball is played by or touches any part of the body of a defender on its way into the goal. As long as it does not leave the striking circle, a goal is still scored. If the ball does leave the circle, it must again be played in the circle by an attacker before entering the goal.

Remember that the lines forming the striking circle are considered part of the circle when a shot is taken.

BULLY

A bully is a way of restarting the game. It can occur when:

- an outfield player's clothing traps the ball
- the ball disintegrates during play
- there is a simultaneous breach of the rules requiring play to stop
- an injury occurs where no penalty is awarded.

During a bully, a player from each side faces the other, with his or her own goal to their right and the ball between them. All other players stand at least 5m (5½ yds) away.

When the whistle is blown, each player taps his or her opponent's stick with his or her stick above the ball, then taps the ground to the right of the ball. After one tap of the stick and ground, the players can play the ball.

Two players restart the game with a bully. A bully may not be played within 14.63m (16 yds) of the backline.

THE RAISED BALL

In open play, the ball can be raised as long as it is not dangerous or leads to a dangerous situation. A ball cannot be raised deliberately from a set piece such as a free hit, or a hit-in from the sideline or corner. It may be allowed to enter the circle in the air providing it does so safely. Only a goalkeeper may play a ball above shoulder height, and then only to stop or deflect it.

The aerial ball

Throwing an aerial ball is a way of sending the ball long distances over the heads of opponents. The ball must be safe on the way up and only received and played to the ground safely by one player who can be from either side. The nearest player to the dropping ball must indicate by name that he or she is in a position to safely and legitimately receive it, and opponents must retreat out of playing distance.

If players of both sides are, or are likely to be, beneath the ball as it falls, a penalty is awarded against the team who raised the ball. The ball is taken from where it was raised. If a player of either team goes to receive an aerial ball but is hindered by an opponent near by, a penalty is awarded against that opponent. It is taken from where the ball lands.

Ashley Jackson throws an aerial ball upwards. The ball must travel upwards safely and be collected by one player.

An outfield player can raise the ball if deemed safe by the match officials.

DEFENDING SHOTS AT GOAL

The goalkeeper should take charge of organising the defence in order to prevent the opposition from shooting. The goalkeeper should command the whole of the circle up to the 23-m (25-yd) line.

Goalkeepers

A goalkeeper may stand or adopt any posture or position to defend shots at goal. This includes lying on the ground, known as logging. Any part of a goalkeeper's body may be used to stop a shot. The legs and feet may be used to propel the ball. The stick can also propel the ball, providing it is below shoulder height. Other parts of the body, including the hand not holding the stick, may be used to stop or deflect the ball but not to propel it.

The goalkeeper may deflect the ball over the crossbar or round the uprights using his or her hand or stick.

FACE MASKS

The four defenders defending a penalty corner may now wear facemasks, only for the duration of the penalty corner. As soon as the ball has either gone out of play, out of the circle or the short corner has broken down, the defenders must remove their face masks.

 The goalkeeper stretches out to make a save.

England's Hilary Rose saves a penalty stroke against New Zealand to give England the bronze medal in the 2006 Commonwealth Games.

Other defenders

Defenders other than goalkeepers have no special privileges when it comes to defending the ball on its way into the goal. A penalty stroke will be awarded against them if:

- they use any part of their bodies accidentally or deliberately to stop or propel the ball

- a deliberate foul is committed by a defending player or the goalkeeper in the circle

- an accidental foul stops a goal.

HANDLING THE BALL

Only goalkeepers are permitted to handle the ball. However, a player may use his or her hand in self-defence for a ball likely to strike his or her body. In such cases, the player would not be penalised, although a penalty might be awarded against the player who raised the ball in the first place.

BALL IN GOALKEEPER'S CLOTHING

If the ball becomes lodged in the goalkeeper's clothing in the striking circle, a penalty corner should be awarded.

FOOT AND BALL CONTACT

Only the stick may be used to strike and play the ball. If a part of the player's body, usually the foot, strikes the ball it is an offence and a penalty is awarded against that player.

If the ball accidentally strikes a player's foot or any other part of his or her body, there is no offence, providing the player could not avoid the contact and no major advantage was gained. If an important advantage was gained, the umpire may award a penalty against the player the ball struck.

UNDERSTANDING THE GAME

To the casual observer, hockey can sometimes appear complex. In fact, it is a simple game once the basic concepts, skills and rules have been learnt and understood.

◀ An attacker (centre) uses a gap between two defenders. The left defender attempts to recover, and the defender on the right engages to delay the attacker.

▶ This diagram shows the three zones of the pitch and the priorities for a team in each zone.

PHASES OF THE GAME

There are two distinct phases in a game of hockey:

- the attacking phase – when one's own team has the ball
- the defending phase – when the opposition has the ball.

In each phase, individuals and the team have important objectives, skills and styles of play. Effective team play depends on individual players understanding the objectives and styles of play as well as mastering and performing the key skills.

PRINCIPLES OF PLAY

The principles behind a team's play depend on whether they are attacking or defending. In attack, teams aim for possession, speed, mobility, width, support and penetration. In defence, team principles are depth, delay, balance, organisation, security and speed.

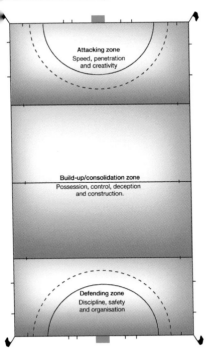

accurate passes. Composure when on the ball is vital, especially when trying to create goal-scoring chances and to convert chances into goals.

DEFENDING OBJECTIVES AND SKILLS

The objectives, for both the individual and the team, when defending are to:

- regain possession of the ball as soon as possible

- 'step up' or 'close down' the forwards and cut off their options to run with the ball or pass

- delay and show patience to regain possession

- deny the opposing team shooting and goal-scoring opportunities in one's own striking circle.

In defending, teams need to be disciplined, organised and secure. Defending players must be able to mark an opponent and to delay, close down and channel opponents as an attack develops. Defenders must be capable of intercepting a loose pass, which is often the first method of gaining possession. Tackling is the last method of regaining possession. They must attempt to prevent and deny goal-scoring opportunities and, in the case especially of the goalkeeper, be able to protect and defend the goal.

ATTACKING OBJECTIVES AND SKILLS

The objectives, for both the individual and the team, when attacking are to:

- keep width, depth and provide support

- contribute to the attack

- maintain shape and position

- run into spaces to receive passes.

In the attacking phase, teams aim for fluid, expansive and creative play. Attacking requires players to be able to control the ball well. They need to be able to run and dribble at different angles, as well as make

BASIC SKILLS

There are three basic factors that underpin the skills of the game. These are the grip (the way the stick is held), footwork and vision.

GRIP

Mastering the correct grip is a vital step in learning and succeeding with other hockey skills. For right-handed players, the left hand holds the top of the stick so that a 'V' is formed by the thumb and forefinger down the back of the stick. This grip will result in the flat (hitting) face of the stick facing the ground. The right hand is placed a third to halfway down the shaft of the stick. Holding the stick in this way is known as open stick.

To turn the stick round to play the ball in the opposite direction is known as reverse stick. The turning movement of the stick from open to reverse stick and back is controlled by the left hand. The right hand adds support and control as the stick is rotated through it. Both hands must feel comfortable when the stick is held in the open and reverse stick position.

◀ This player shows a good grip and body position as he moves with the ball ahead of himself but under close control.

FOOTWORK

Players must learn to move forwards, sideways and backwards while maintaining close control of the ball with their stick head. Good footwork will increase a player's mobility and balance. It is crucial for players to have their feet in the direction in which they are going. It is also absolutely essential in creating space and time when under pressure, and also being balanced to execute a skill.

VISION AND POSITIONING

When in control of the ball, a player must be able to see as much as possible of what is occurring over the rest of the pitch. As the player moves with the ball, the position of his or her body compared to the ball will affect what he or she can see. If the ball is kept too close to the feet, the player's body and head will inevitably be bent over the ball and his vision reduced accordingly.

A good body position involves the player's upper body being angled forward with the head up. The stick position ensures the ball is held in front of and slightly to the right of the body. A leading left elbow will assist in a good body position for ball carrying. In this position, the player should have an excellent view of what is happening around them.

Coaching of these basic skills should focus around positions of the body (including the head), the feet and the ball.

A good grip technique. Some players like to extend the index finger of their right hand down the shaft, but young players should avoid this for safety reasons.

Whenever you can, work on moving in different directions at different speeds but always keeping the ball under close control.

ATTACKING PLAY

Attacking play calls on players to exhibit a wide range of skills including ball control, dribbling and passing. It also requires players to run with the ball, moving the ball along with simple movements of the stick. Players creating space by moving off the ball (leading and releading) is crucial to the game.

CONTROLLING THE BALL

Control and composure are essential when players are attempting to keep possession of the ball in a game. This is especially the case when they are being pressured by opponents.

RUNNING WITH THE BALL

Good technique should allow a player to look up and assess the situation before choosing his or her next move, be it a pass, eliminating an opponent, a dribble or a shot.

Running with the ball is most effective when there is plenty of time and space to operate and when there are no opponents near by. If the player shows good pace, control and awareness, though, he or she may be able to eliminate and beat an opponent.

Ask your coach for practices and games, which allow you to practise the techniques of eliminating a player using feinting and dummying.

▶ Running forward at pace, the player keeps his head up to check on the space he plans to run into.

Technique

1. Hold the body with the back as straight as possible, with the stick held at the top with the left hand.

2. The stick and ball should be kept well out in front of the body and slightly to the right. This makes it easier to look up whilst running at speed.

3. Good footwork is essential to allow you to move forward yet stay balanced.

4. The player needs the ability to look or 'scan' ahead so that he or she can read the pattern of play. Players must learn to recognise when they should pass or when they should run with the ball.

DRIBBLING

Dribbling is moving with the ball, either keeping stick-ball contact or using a series of short and repeated taps or drags of the ball. Once mastered, it allows a player to attempt more complex skills, such as eliminating a player (a move designed to trick an opponent into moving in one direction so you can pass them with the ball in another), feinting (providing a misleading movement designed to distract an opponent) and dummying (using the stick/body to disguise a movement).

Technique

1. Dribbling involves open and reverse stick positions as the ball is moved from left to right. This is achieved by rolling the hands and wrists.

2. The left hand controls the twisting, rotational movement of the stick. The right hand generates the pulling and pushing action necessary for moving the ball. The right hand also provides control and stability.

3. Young players should first learn to move the ball from open to reverse stick with a small amount of movement. Once mastered, they can build up their pace through walking, jogging and, finally, running at speed.

 A player dribbles past his opponent's reverse-stick side.

1 v 1 ELIMINATION SKILLS TECHNIQUE

1. Maintain a low and balanced body position when moving with the ball.

2. Run quickly on angle to commit the defender.

3. Prepare for the drag at least a stick's distance from the defender.

4. Transfer the ball with a drag from one side to the other (various angles may be used as appropriate).

5. Accelerate to eliminate the defender.

EXECUTING LOW LIFTS

1. Prepare early.

2. Lower your body weight.

3. Generally keep the left foot forward if it is an open lift.

4. Generally keep the right foot forward if it is a reverse lift.

5. Keep the ball in front, out of reach of the defender.

6. Keep the stick at 45 degrees with the face upwards.

7. Lift underneath the ball gently with the right hand.

8. Ensure the ball only lifts a maximum of 50cm (20 in) from the ground and is safe.

PASSING

Passing links individuals' play and is absolutely fundamental to a team's success. You should practise as often as possible.

A pass involves two players – the passer and the receiver. There needs to be awareness and understanding between the two in order for a pass to be completed successfully. In addition, the passer must be aware of the positions of team-mates and opponents, remain balanced and have control of the ball. These three factors – awareness, balance and control – are often known as the ABC of passing.

The player alters her grip and brings her left foot and shoulder forward to execute a push pass.

Hit
Used for passing the ball quickly over long distances, for shooting at goal, and when taking free hits or hits-in from the side- and backline.

Push
The most commonly used pass in the game. It is not as fast or powerful a pass as the hit, but the push tends to be a more accurate type of pass.

Reverse push
Used most often over short distances when passing from left to right and when there is no suitable open-stick pass. Usually played square or behind square.

Slap
Similar to the push pass, but the stroke is made with more force and can result in long, powerful passes.

Flick
An extension of the push pass. It is used to lift the ball into the air in a range of situations, from making a long, overhead pass, to taking a shot over a defender's stick or a goalkeeper lying on the ground.

Aerial
An alternative pass where there is a change in grip and body position. The basic grip is used, and a low body position is required, with a step into the ball. The ball should be in front of the left foot, and the player should stand side-on to the target line. The stick head should smoothly accelerate upwards once in contact with the ball, and just before release, lever the left hand down against the right hand for power.

▼ After hitting the ball this player transfers her weight from the back to the front foot and follows through with the stick.

All these skills require hours of practice, which can be done on your own.

RECEIVING THE BALL

Instant control of the ball is essential for the receiver and the first touch is crucial. If the receiver controls the ball then extra time and space are likely to be created in which the player can prepare for and make his or her next move.

When receiving the ball, the open or reverse stick will be used, depending on where the ball is received and what action the player has to or wants to take next. Sometimes, the receiver will want to stop the ball dead. Most often, though, he or she will want the ball under control and will reposition it ready for his or her next move, which could be a pass, shot, dribble or run with the ball.

Players must learn to receive and get the ball under control in as little time as possible.

> **Always follow up your own and your team-mates' shots on goal. There is a chance that a rebound will leave you with another chance to score.**

A player celebrates scoring a goal.

SHOOTING AND GOAL-SCORING

Whilst spectacular goals are fun to score, the simplest of goals count just as much. Good goal-scorers – often the team's strikers – not only know how to shoot, but also when to shoot and when to pass to a team-mate in a more favourable position.

All shots on goal should be on target. Saved shots often provide rebounds from the goalkeeper, the goalposts, or from a defender's stick which, in turn, can lead to a second chance for a strike on goal.

Many goal-scoring opportunities appear suddenly and awkwardly. High levels of concentration and sound technical ability are required to take advantage of these half-chances when they arise.

A goal-scorer's attributes

To become a top goal-scorer requires high levels of desire, determination, courage and commitment to succeed. Good strikers must be prepared to chase lost causes, get on the end of crosses, pick up deflections and collect passes that arrive at different heights and angles. They must also be able to control the ball and make a shot at goal, often under pressure from defenders, and in the minimum time and space available.

A player receives the ball using a reverse stick position.

DEFENDING PLAY

The team with the ball aims to keep possession long enough to launch an attack and score. The defending team's main aims are to prevent attackers from scoring, and to regain possession of the ball so that they can start an attack themselves.

REGAINING POSSESSION

Generally, possession is regained in three ways:

1. by putting pressure on the attacking players
2. by intercepting badly timed and mis-directed passes
3. by tackling an opponent who is in possession of the ball.

INTERCEPTING

Interceptions rely on the defenders' abilities to read the game, marking opponents closely and anticipating their actions. The intercepting player must watch the ball carefully, and move towards the ball with the stick down on the ground. He or she must then move away quickly with the ball or pass once possession has been made.

When making an open-stick tackle, try to position yourself goal side and to the right of the attacker before attempting the tackle.

A player must be balanced and adopt a strong base, with the left foot leading and the right leg trailing to execute an open-side block tackle.

TACKLING

The aim of tackling is to regain possession, although it is sometimes used to put the ball out of play to give time for the tackler's team to reorganise their defence. The main points to remember when tackling are:

- watch the ball, not the stick or the body of the player in possession

- time the tackle correctly; don't be tempted to dive in

- recognise when to tackle and which tackle to use

- channel the attacking player on to his reverse-stick side (the defender's open-stick side).

CHANNELLING

Channelling is the action of a defender preventing an attacker entering space, usually a direct line to goal. The main points to remember are:

- channelling is achieved by good footwork

- adopt a sideways position

- keep the stick fairly close to the ground

- get the body into a position to prevent the attacker driving towards goal and cutting back with the ball to pass infield.

There are three main types of tackle:

1. Jab
The jab can be executed with speed and surprise. The stick is held in the left hand and is lunged rapidly at the ball like the head of a striking snake. The right hand may be used occasionally to provide support just before making the tackle. Ideally the left leg can lead to allow a longer reach, but the defender must try to stay on his or her toes. This allows quick movement forwards or backwards if the first tackle is unsuccessful.

2. Open stick
This is the most commonly used tackle and can be performed when on the move or standing still. The left foot leads the tackling movement. The right foot provides the support required to change direction if the first attempt fails. If performed when standing still, the stick is nearly always used as a barrier to perform a block tackle. When performed on the move, a more upright stick position is used.

 A player attempts a reverse stick tackle.

3. Reverse stick

Players are not allowed to make contact with an opponent's body or stick. So, defenders have to get into a position where they can make the tackle level with, or in front of, their own body. Usually, this tackle is one-handed, although occasionally, it can be made, two-handed. The further away from the defender that the tackle is made, the flatter the stick must be to the ground. Tackles made with flat sticks are more effective when playing on artificial surfaces or indoors.

MARKING

Marking means tracking individual players and covering space through which passes can be made. It is an important aspect of the game as it is crucial in defenders' attempts to stop the attacker gaining possession of the ball.

- Marking will generally be from the side or slightly in front for most of the pitch, with the defender trying to intercept the ball.

- Marking an attacker in the circle will generally be from slightly behind the player or to the side if more experienced, with the defender trying to intercept the ball.

The defender will keep close to the attacker and remain between the attacker and the goal.

There are three main methods of organising a team's defence:

- person-to-person marking (one-to-one)
- zonal marking
- a combination of both.

Person-to-person marking

When the opposition have the ball each player from the defending team marks an assigned opponent.

Zonal marking

In this system defending players form a zone as soon as their team loses possession. Each defender takes responsibility for any opponent who comes into his or her zone of defence. The zone concentrates and tightens marking in the area of greatest danger. Discipline and maintaining organisation and communication between defenders is critical to the system's success.

Combination marking systems

The most effective marking systems are those which use a combination of zonal and person-to-person marking. This style uses tight person-to-person marking of opponents close to the ball, with the rest of the defence employing zonal marking.

The crucial moment for the team is when possession is lost. Failure to react quickly can allow the attacking side to gain numerical superiority (more attackers than defenders) in the danger area and penetrate the defence's circle.

SYSTEMS OF PLAY

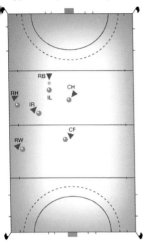

In a person-to-person marking system, the defending team's players (red triangles) each get close to members of the opposition (blue circles).

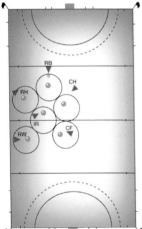

In a zonal marking system, defenders cover an area of the pitch and mark any opponent entering their area.

The 5-3-2 system operates with a left back, right back, left half, centre half, right half, left wing, left inside, centre forward, right inside and right wing.

The 4-4-2 system operates with a left half, centre back, sweeper, right half, left midfield, two centre midfields (one of which may act as a support forward), right midfield, and left and right forwards.

The 4-3-3 system operates with a left half, centre back, sweeper, right half, left midfield, centre midfield, right midfield, left foward, centre forward and right forward.

The 3-3-1-3 system operates with a centre back, left half, sweeper, right half, left midfield, centre midfield, right midfield, left forward, centre forward and right forward.

GOALKEEPING

The goalkeeper's role is to protect the goal. All goalkeeping actions should start from the balanced ready position, which can be used as a springboard for any move.

Low shots

Low shots directed straight at the goalkeeper should be stopped with the kickers or leg pads. Then the ball should be kicked out of danger towards the sidelines, for safety, and never back through the middle of the circle.

Save-clear kicking technique

- The kick is executed by the foot on the side to which the goalkeeper is clearing (left foot, left side and right foot, right side).

- The goalkeeper steps forwards towards the ball and balances on the first foot (step forward on the left foot for a right-side clear and the right foot for a left-side clear).

- Turn the hips slightly towards the direction of the kick.

- The kick is made with the inside of the kicker, and contact with the ball is made for as long as possible.

- Keep the head over the ball as the kick is made.

- Follow through so that both feet come together in the HOKOA position (see handy hint, right).

Often the goalkeeper will need to make saves using his or her stick or hand. When the ball is in the air, the hand should be used. If the ball is beyond the reach of the goalkeeper's hands, the stick can be used.

Hand saves

- The goalkeeper should aim to cushion the ball so it falls vertically to the ground.

- The goalkeeper then uses the feet to save clear – kicking the ball away to start an attacking move.

- If the ball is above waist-height, point the fingers upwards.

- If the ball is below waist-height, point the fingers downwards.

Ask your coach for practices to develop the HOKOA (Head, Over Knees, Over Ankles) goalkeeping technique.

A goalkeeper must stay alert throughout the game. Quick reactions and good footwork can get them in position in time to clear the ball or make a save.

Stick saves

- Where possible the gloved hand should move across the body – under the chin or above the eyes (so as not to impede vision).

- The stick in the right hand can be placed behind the gloved hand to support the save – particularly effective with a hard shot.

- The goalkeeper may save the ball wide at any height with the stick.

Commanding the defence

All good goalkeepers must know how to command the circle, both physically and vocally. They should not be afraid of marshalling the defence, and they should always look to be not only the last line of defence, but also the launching pad of many attacks. Goalkeepers are not permitted to enter their opponent's half of the pitch, except specifically to take a penalty stroke.

Goalkeeping equipment

Advances in goalkeeping equipment have been made in recent years. Today the wide range of protective equipment available includes:

- helmet and strong visor
- throat protector
- chest pad
- shoulder and elbow pads
- gloves
- abdominal protector
- genital protector
- padded shorts and thigh protectors
- lightweight leg-guards
- knee pads
- lightweight kickers
- boots or other suitable footwear.

As a goalkeeper, work really hard and get coaching help to develop fast, balanced footwork. Good footwork helps set you up to make successful saves.

RESTARTS AND SET PIECES

Every game contains a large number of stoppages. Restarts and set pieces are a major part of the game. They should be learnt, practised and perfected in order to gain maximum advantage from them.

A player takes a long swing to hit a powerful free hit.

COMMON RESTARTS

The most common restart and set piece situations are:

- free hits
- hits-in from the sideline
- hits-in from the backline
- penalty corners.

FREE HITS

To gain maximum advantage from a free hit, the team in possession should attempt to take it as quickly as possible, before the defending team has had the time to reorganise. If a quick, effective free-hit opportunity is not available, a team may use a routine they have worked on in training.

Do not gamble on a risky target; keep possession and try to move the ball into your opponents' danger areas or circle. Consider also that the player on the ball decides what happens, but the players off the ball dictate what happens next.

Hits-in from the sideline apply the same principles and objectives as a free hit.

HITS-IN FROM A CORNER

Opportunities to take quick hits-in from a corner are rare because the defending team usually has time to reorganise itself. Attacking players should manoeuvre themselves so that they are both free to receive the ball and can receive it on their open-stick side. With the ball, they look to attack the reverse-stick side of their marker.

Defending players are expected to counter every move by the attacking side and prevent the ball being received by the attackers in the danger areas. The goalkeeper is the key defender. The team defence should always allow the goalkeeper to have a clear view of the ball.

SHORT PASS TACTICS

Try to adopt the following format:

- principles – what are we trying to do?

- roles – what are the roles of each player within this?

- rules – what rules apply?

- options – what alternatives are there?

SUPPORT FOR A SHORT PASS

At a short pass from a corner, an attacker may play the ball short to a team-mate close by. The aim is to try to move a well-organised defence around and then work it into the danger areas. Defending sides should be alert for short passes from the sideline and give the task of closing down the player with the ball to specific defenders.

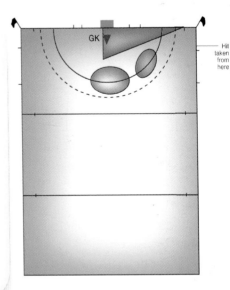

Hit taken from here

This diagram shows the danger areas, which an attacking team should target from a long corner.

PENALTY CORNERS

The penalty corner is a unique aspect of the game. The rules of hockey place important restrictions on both attacking and defending sides when a penalty corner is taken (see pages 46–47).

Attacking

There are three components to the attacking penalty corner.

1. Injection – putting the ball in play from the backline.

2. Stopping – the ball is no longer required to be stopped, but some teams will still do this.

3. Shooting – accurate and on target.

The aim is to score a goal by a direct shot, rebound or pass that will lead to a shot. A variety of options are important, but it is better to have a few well-practised routines, rather than a large number that do not work.

The attacking team always has the advantage at penalty corners, as the defending team has to react to the attacking side's move. Defending teams can only try to anticipate what is going to happen.

This diagram shows the danger zones from a penalty corner. The hatched areas are zones the attacking unit can exploit for deflections.

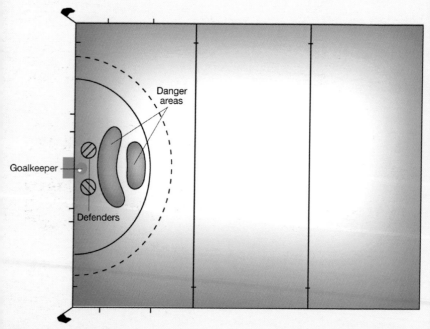

Defending

Only four players and the goalkeeper are allowed to defend the penalty corner. No such limitation is placed on the numbers that the attacking team can employ. The problem that the defence has is how to deploy five players to cover all the options available to the attack (see pages 40–41).

At set pieces such as these, the goalkeeper is the key defender and will advise the defenders where to stand and where to run. He or she must always be allowed clear sight of the ball – goalkeepers have the protective equipment and skills to deal effectively with powerful, direct shots at goal.

SMOTHERING A SHOT

Top class goalkeepers feel confident enough in their ability, as well as the quality of their protective equipment, to use their entire bodies to smother and save shots at goal. This is an advanced skill and should not be attempted by a novice goalkeeper as it might result in injury.

The defending team's five players are ready to run out to defend against a penalty corner. They are focused on either covering the goal or running out to challenge, intercept or block a shot.

Defence at penalty corners

In general, the following patterns form the basis of most defending at penalty corners. Penalty defence will depend on the level of game being played. This scenario may be ideal for a school team, and there are many variations that will be used at different levels, and especially at higher levels of play (see diagrams 1 to 4).

1. Player **A** sprints out to exert pressure on the striker and aims to:

- hurry the striker into the shot to try to force a mistake

- prevent the shot being taken

- take a running line out that allows the striker to play the ball with the open stick, while covering any possibility of passes into other areas

- be prepared to slow down if it is obvious that the attackers are not going to strike straight away or if the ball is passed to another striker

- be prepared to assist the other members of the defence in repelling further phases of the attack.

2. Player **B** runs to the left of player **A**, and slightly behind and aims to:

- cover and intercept any passes to attackers in and around the striking circle

- take the additional responsibility of dealing with rebounds, knock-downs off the goalkeeper or any other player.

3. Players **C** and **D** each have responsibility for the areas on either side of the goalkeeper and near to the goal posts. Sometimes, player **D** is deployed in a position alongside and to the right of the goalkeeper. In this position, he or she is expected to cover any passes into an area to the right of and behind player **A**. Rebounds, knock-downs and deflections off and around the goalkeeper to the keeper's right-hand side will also be player **D**'s responsibility.

Player D Player A Goalkeeper Player B Player C

The four outfield defenders plus their goalkeeper line up for a penalty corner.

4. The goalkeeper usually takes up a position covering the middle parts of the goal, but in advance of players **C** and **D**. This position may be 2–6m (6½–19½ ft) off the goal line. Some goalkeepers come as far as possible off their goal line in order to narrow the angle of the shot and to exert pressure on the striker. But this move comes at a risk. The closer to the shot the goalkeeper is, the less time he or she has to react to it.

> As a goalkeeper, the further off the goal line you are at a penalty corner, the more vulnerable your goal is to a shot from a wide position.

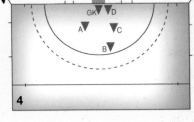

Defensive short corner start and running-out positions: **1)** 2-2 start, **2)** 2-2 run out, **3)** 3-1 start, and **4)** 3-1 run out.

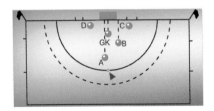

This diagram shows the usual positions aimed for by the defending players moving out once a penalty corner has been taken.

PENALTIES

There are two forms of penalty in hockey – match penalties and personal penalties. Including advantage, there are six types of match penalties, whilst there are four different forms of personal penalty.

MATCH PENALTIES

Free hit

This is the normal penalty for a basic offence, such as kicking the ball, raising the ball dangerously or barging. It is a hit or push awarded by the umpire to the team against which the offence has occurred. A free hit can be awarded anywhere on the pitch, except when a defending team commits an offence in its own striking circle.

 The umpire signals to restart the game after a goal has been scored.

Advance 10 metres

This may be awarded when, after already awarding a free hit, the umpire spots a further offence. Typical offences at a free hit are showing dissent or arguing with the umpire's decision, picking up the ball to delay the free hit or deliberately not retreating 5m (5½ yds) away from the free hit position. In these situations, the umpire directs that the free hit may be advanced 10m (11 yds). The team taking the free hit have the choice of advancing the ball forward or not. However, if a 10-m advance would take the free

hit into their opponent's striking circle, then the umpire increases the award to a penalty corner.

Reverse the free hit

Certain offences at a free hit may result in the umpire reversing his or her award and giving the free hit to the team who originally offended. One example of such an offence is where a striker of a free hit delays it long enough for team-mates to get into better positions.

Penalty corner

A penalty corner is awarded against a defending team for:

- a deliberate offence within its own 23-m (25-yd) area, but outside the striking circle

- an unintentional offence inside its own circle that prevents a possible goal or denies an attacker actual or likely possession of the ball

- a deliberate offence by a defender inside the circle against an opponent not in possession or likely to gain the ball.

The last of these awards must be accompanied by some form of personal penalty for misconduct (see page 50).

Penalty stroke

This is awarded for:

- a deliberate or unintentional breach of the rules by the defence that prevents a likely goal being scored

- a deliberate breach of the rules by the defence that deprives an attacker of actual or likely possession of the ball

- persistent illegal crossing of the backline by the defenders at a penalty corner.

An umpire awards a free hit to the defending team.

Application of advantage

Advantage occurs when an umpire chooses not to blow the whistle for an offence. Instead, the umpire signals and may call to the players for them to play on. The point of applying advantage is to reduce any benefit the offending team may get from a halt in play and the award of a match penalty. This usually involves the side offended against keeping possession of the ball. Play can often be allowed to proceed and then, dependent on the outcome, the umpire can decide whether or not to ignore the previous offence or bring play to a halt and award a match penalty where the offence occurred.

Advantage can apply to all the normal match penalties. Signalling advantage is important not only for distant players to continue positional play, but also so that the other umpire is aware of what is happening.

MATCH PENALTY PROCEDURE

Free hit

The umpire blows the whistle and raises an arm with palm outstretched, at shoulder height and in the direction of the hit. The hit or push is taken on or near the spot where the offence took place with as little delay as possible. Opposition players should be at least 5m (5½ yds) away.

When a free hit is awarded to the attacking team within 5m (5½ yds) of the defending team's circle, all players of both teams (other than the free hit striker) must be at least 5m (5½ yds) from the ball. If the attackers infringe, a free hit is awarded to the defence. If the defence infringes, a penalty corner is awarded.

Advance 10 metres

The umpire blows the whistle and holds up an arm above the head, with fist clenched. The team taking the free hit may move the ball forwards for a distance up to 10m (11 yds).

Reverse the free hit

The umpire blows the whistle and indicates in the opposite direction to the original free hit. Such an award is normally accompanied by an explanation from the umpire as to why his or her decision has been reversed.

An umpire signals clearly that he is playing advantage.

Remember that the umpire may play advantage during the game. Even when you are sure an offence has been committed, play on until you hear the whistle.

 An umpire signalling a 16-yd (14-m) hit.

Penalty corner procedure

1. The umpire blows the whistle and signals a penalty corner (holds both arms straight in front of the body, pointing towards the goal with palms facing each other).

2. Up to five defenders move behind their backline and the remainder beyond the centre line. The supporting umpire moves into the control umpire's half.

3. The ball is placed on or beyond the 10-m (11-yd) line on the backline. Defenders behind the backline remain at least 5m (5½ yds) clear of the ball.

4. The injector sets up to inject the ball, having at least one foot outside the field. The remaining attackers take position outside the circle. The attacking team can position any of its 10 outfield players, but not the goalkeeper, in attack.

5. When ready, the attacker on the backline hits or pushes the ball. No goal can be scored directly from this strike.

6. As soon as the ball is moved, the defenders may leave the backline and the attackers may enter the circle. If the defenders move too early and gain advantage, the umpire may order it to be retaken. If this breaking is persistent, a penalty stroke may be awarded. If the attackers move too early, a free hit is awarded to the defending team.

7. The ball may be played by either or both teams anywhere outside the circle, but must be played on the ground outside the circle before a shot at goal is taken from inside the circle.

8. If the first shot at goal is a hit, there are rules regarding deflections mainly to do with safety. The ball must cross the goal line or be heading on a path that will take it across the goal line before any deflection by any player occurs. This deflection must be no higher than the backboard 46cm (18 in) at the point of crossing the goal line, unless it touches a defender's stick or body during its travel.

9. For any other type of shot at goal, and for subsequent hits, the ball may be raised to any height, subject to there being no actual or likely danger.

10. A penalty stroke is awarded if a defender (other than the goalkeeper) remains in the goal and stops the ball from entering the goal with his or her body.

11. If the ball travels beyond 5m (5½ yds) from the circle, the penalty corner is ended.

12. A penalty corner awarded at the end of time for a half is still taken but ends if the ball passes out of the circle a second time.

 An umpire directing a free hit.

The attacking team prepares to execute a short-corner routine.

The penalty stroke

1. The umpire blows the whistle, raises one arm vertically and points to the penalty spot with the other arm.

2. Time is stopped by both umpires and, if required, by match officials.

3. The goalkeeper moves to take up position with parts of both of his or her feet on the goal line.

4. The striker – who may be any outfield player or the attacking team's goalkeeper – places the ball on the penalty spot. He or she takes up position behind the ball, ready to shoot.

5. All non-participating players retire beyond the 23-m (25-yd) line.

6. The support umpire, having checked where non-participating players are, takes up position on the backline some 10m (11 yds) from goal. The control umpire takes up position behind and slightly to the right of the striker.

7. The control umpire checks with the striker and the goalkeeper that each is ready to start, then the whistle is blown to take the stroke.

8. The striker may push (not drag), flick or lift the ball, touching it once only, to any height towards goal. The ball may not be hit, nor may the striker feint at playing the ball.

9. The striker may take one step forward. The rear foot may not pass the front one until the ball has been played.

10. If a goal is scored, the umpire blows the whistle and signals a goal. The teams move into their own halves ready for the game to restart.

11. The umpire blows the whistle to start and end the stroke. The umpire will blow the whistle to end the stroke if:

- a goal is scored
- a goal is not scored
- the ball comes to rest inside the circle
- the ball is caught in the goalkeeper's leg-guard
- the ball is caught by the goalkeeper
- the ball passes outside the circle
- the stroke-taker breaches one of the rules of hockey.

The teams prepare for the game to restart with a defensive hit 14.63m (16 yds) in front of the centre of the goal line.

12. If the defending goalkeeper breaches any rule that prevents a goal from being scored, the umpire blows the whistle and awards a penalty goal. The teams then take up positions to restart the game from the centre line.

13. Time and the game restarts when both umpires and the teams are in position and the controlling umpire blows his or her whistle.

An Australian player takes a penalty stroke against the Malaysian goalkeeper during the 2006 Commonwealth Games.

An umpire showing
a green card.

PERSONAL PENALTIES

Personal penalties are used to deal
with players' misconduct. They
usually follow the umpire awarding
a match penalty. Four different
types of personal penalty exist:

- a caution
- a warning (green card awarded)
- a temporary suspension
  (yellow card awarded)
- a permanent suspension
  (red card awarded).

PERSONAL PENALTY
PROCEDURE

Rough or dangerous play or any
other form of misconduct should be
dealt with by a match penalty, if
appropriate, and may also see the
award of a personal penalty. If the
umpire chooses to play advantage,
then a personal penalty might be
awarded at the first available
stoppage after, and not at the time
of, the offence. Green, yellow and
red cards are recommended for use
if available, but personal penalties
can still be given without them.
A player who has received a
warning or temporary suspension
for a specific offence may not be
awarded the same personal penalty
for a repetition of that offence.

Caution
A caution normally sees the
umpire signal or talk to the player
concerned briefly about his or her
behaviour. Sometimes, it can be
done without stopping the game.
It can simply take the form of a
loud whistle and a warning sign
accompanied by a clear facial
expression from the umpire.

A caution might also be given to
one or both captains to exercise
responsibility for their teams more
effectively. If this is done, the game
should be stopped so that the
umpire can talk to the captain or
captains. Time should be allowed
for the captain or captains to
communicate the umpire's
message to their teams.

Warning

The game should be stopped for a warning and, if necessary, a check made with match officials that they can see what is happening. The offending player(s) should be called to stand in front of the umpire who may then explain what the warning is for. The umpire should write down:

- the time of the event
- the number(s) of the player(s) concerned
- a brief note of the reason.

When this is done, the player(s) should be invited to turn so that the umpire's colleague and the match official can also see the player number(s) and record the event. The offending player(s) may then return to their positions and the match is then restarted.

A warning from the umpire is just that, a warning about your play. Follow his or her advice in order to avoid receiving a stronger penalty.

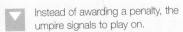

Instead of awarding a penalty, the umpire signals to play on.

Temporary suspension

A temporary suspension (usually signalled with a yellow card) lasts for a minimum of 5 minutes. A suspended player is sent from the field to the care of a match official, if one is appointed, or to the corner of the pitch at the player's defending end.

As a courtesy, the umpire indicates to his/her colleague and to the offender's team captain how long the suspension should last. Whilst under suspension, the player must remain silent but may be given water and protective clothing. If the player is not silent or there is other continuing misconduct, the suspension may be lengthened. Once the player has completed a temporary suspension, he or she may return to the pitch. Alternatively, the team may choose to substitute him and send on a replacement.

Permanent suspension

This is used by the umpire to deal with particularly unpleasant offences, often involving violence. It is indicated by the use of a red card. The suspended player must leave the pitch immediately and cannot re-enter at any point during the game. In many countries, the penalty does not stop there and the player may be banned from playing one or more further games.

The Australia women's team put pressure on the India women's goal in the 2006 Commonwealth Games.

Two umpires consult each other before giving a decision.

Suspension of goalkeepers

A game of hockey can go on even if one or both sides do not have a fully-equipped goalkeeper playing. Therefore, if a goalkeeper is suspended, it is not necessary to play a substitute goalkeeper. However, a team can substitute one of their outfield players for their reserve goalkeeper on the substitutes bench. The substitution can last the length of the suspension.

When a team does not have a substitute goalkeeper, the umpire can make time for an outfield player to put on the right equipment (at the minimum, a helmet and shirt of a different colour) and play as the goalkeeper for the length of the suspension.

THE NATIONAL DISCIPLINARY CODE

In England, a permanent suspension is covered by the National Disciplinary Code. This requires that the player be automatically suspended from playing, coaching or umpiring for at least 16 days. The suspension period can be longer and depends on the actual offence and the umpire's red card report form.

CONTROL OF THE GAME

Two umpires are appointed to control a game and uphold the rules of hockey. At some higher level games, match officials assist umpires by taking on some tasks.

THE UMPIRES

Umpires are often in charge of timing the game and all its other rules. They should be dressed similarly in shirts of the same colour and with black trousers/skirts and socks of the same colour. The wearing of peaked hats should be normally restricted to keeping the sun or rain out of the eyes, so that their faces can be seen at all times. Whilst umpiring, umpires should carry:

- a current rule book
- a whistle and spare whistle
- a stopwatch
- a pencil and card on which to record goals scored and any players cautioned, warned or suspended.

Umpires should also take to the game:

- a stick ring (to check and ensure that the sticks do not exceed the thickness of the inside circumference of the stick ring – as some players use tape on the bottom of the stick shaft to aid grip in trapping the ball)
- string to repair goal nets around the goalposts
- black insulating tape to repair goal nets
- scissors to cut string and tape.

Umpires must cover a lot of ground in a game and be able to concentrate for its entire duration. They have to be fit, especially at the higher levels where they must pass fitness tests every season.

Umpires have to be fit and focused to keep up with play and make the right decisions.

An umpire's responsibilities

Umpires use signals and a whistle to indicate decisions to start and stop the game, to award goals and match penalties. They also signal when the ball goes out of play and how the game should be restarted.

Each umpire is essentially in charge of a half of the pitch and they do not change ends at half-time. In reality, the area in which an umpire is responsible for decision making includes a slice of the other umpire's half (see diagram below). Each umpire, though, has exclusive responsibility for the award and control of corners, penalty corners, penalty strokes and goals in his or her own half, end and striking circle.

The umpires act as a team before and throughout a game. An umpire may not award a penalty corner, penalty stroke or goal in the other half of the pitch. But he or she may be called upon for their view to help the other umpire.

MATCH OFFICIALS

An independent match official may be appointed to higher level games, whilst tournaments may see a tournament director with technical officers and judges. Their duties can range from checking team lists and players' equipment to recording the timing of the match. A reserve umpire may also be appointed to take over from one of the umpires should he or she suffer an injury or some other problem.

The approximate areas of each umpire's control. The red shaded areas show the area in which the umpires move in. The blue dotted line shows how responsibility on the pitch is approximately divided up between the two umpires.

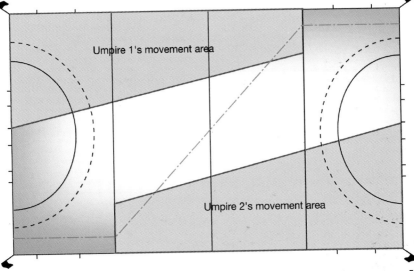

Umpire 1's movement area

Umpire 2's movement area

HOCKEY VARIATIONS

England Hockey runs different versions of hockey for young people and players with special needs. Also, England Hockey has developed a programme called Stix Skills for young people.

STIX SKILLS

The Stix Skills Awards are a fun way of finding out just how good your hockey skills are. The awards are for anyone under 14 years old and there are four levels – Cub, Bronze, Silver and Gold. Participants complete six skills tests, gaining points for skills such as scoring goals, dribbling around cones and lifting the ball over a stick. Points for all the tests are added up giving you a final score – all participants receive a certificate and a badge for the level achieved.

MINI HOCKEY

Mini hockey is a 7-a-side game played across half of a full-sized hockey pitch. The smaller teams and adapted playing areas ensure a type of involvement in the game that will give children great enjoyment and success. Girls and boys can participate side by side in what is a high scoring, fast moving, fun game of hockey.

The mini hockey format provides an ideal stepping stone for young players as they progress towards

 Girls playing mini hockey.

the full game of hockey. England Hockey has a National Mini Hockey Competition that any school or club in the country can enter. Teams play in county, regional and national rounds.

The rules of mini hockey are similar to 11-a-side, but have a few changes to make it safer, quicker and easier for younger players to play. England Hockey is also developing a game specifically for under 11s, in which a team will have six players, with four active at any one time. Teams will be overseen by a young leader/teacher/coach, and the game can be played on a netball court or a quarter of a hockey pitch. Further information is available on the England Hockey website; click on the Young People link.

ZONE HOCKEY

Zone hockey is an adapted version of hockey that can include players of all abilities. It offers opportunities for integration with the able bodied. Girls and boys, both disabled (suitable for electric wheelchair users, manual wheelchair users, ambulant and semi-ambulant youngsters) or non-disabled, can participate side by side. It is a 5-a-side game and can be played both outside on a hard surface, on a quarter of an artificial turf pitch, or inside a sports hall.

Again, the combination of smaller teams and adapted playing areas allow children to have great fun.

Disabled players participate in a game of zone hockey.

GLOSSARY

Aerial ball Throwing an aerial ball is a way of sending the ball long distances over the heads of opponents. The ball must be safe on the way up and only received and played to the ground safely by one player, who can be from either side.

Artificial turf Synthetic nylon-based floor surface. Three types of pitch exist: sand-based, sand-dressed and water-based. Each of these has its own playing characteristics.

Backline Line which marks the end of the pitch where the goal is situated.

Bully Way of restarting the game when an outfield player's clothing traps the ball; the ball disintegrates during play; there is a simultaneous breach of the rules requiring play to stop; or an injury occurs where no penalty is awarded.

Channelling Action of a defending player preventing an attacker entering space, usually a direct line to goal.

Control umpire Although main umpiring responsibility is within each half, in normal practice an umpire's control area is from the far edge of the inner circle diagonally to the near edge of the other umpire's circle.

Covering A player free behind the 'action' ready to step in if required to take the ball.

Dribbling Moving with the ball using a series of short and repeated taps or drags of the ball.

Elimination The act of getting past the opposition.

Feint Providing a misleading movement designed to distract an opponent.

Free hit Given to a team after their opponents have committed an offence, and taken where the offence took place, with minimum delay.

Intercepting Gathering up the opposition's poor passes. Often created by pressure applied from the team not in possession of the ball.

Long corner A free hit taken from near the corner flag. Given for an infringement by a defending player outside of the striking circle. Also, can be given for unintentional infringements inside the circle.

Marking Tracking individual players and covering space through which passes can be made.

Match officials Independent match officials may be appointed to high level games, usually at National League matches and above. Duties may include checking of team lists and player's equipment, timing of matches, recording match events and general liaison with local personnel.

Match penalties Consists of six types and constitutes an accidental or deliberate infringement of the rules.

Open stick When the flat side of the stick faces the ground. The correct grip for open-stick technique involves the left hand at the top of the stick with the thumb and forefinger forming a 'V' down the back of the stick. This will result in the flat (hitting) face of the stick facing the ground. The right hand is placed a third to halfway down the shaft of the stick.

Penalty corner (Sometimes known as a short corner). Two processes exist: attacking penalty corner, whereby it is possible for the attacking team to have a direct shot at goal, and the defensive penalty corner, whereby four defenders and a goalkeeper attempt to deny the penalty-corner-takers a goal-scoring opportunity.

Penalty stroke Taken from the spot in the circle. One attacking player flicks the ball towards the goal, and the goalkeeper tries to save it.

Personal penalties Used to deal with misconduct by players, and a match penalty will nearly always follow.

Reverse stick Technique used when receiving or passing on the open (flat) side is not appropriate.

Scanning Ability to use vision to read patterns of play whilst moving with or manipulating the ball.

Short corner Given against a defending team whoever committed an infringement in the striking circle, for example, either the ball striking a defender's foot or a bad stick tackle by a defender on an attacker's stick.

Striking circle Known either as the circle or 'D', and is 14.63m (16 yds) wide. Goals can only be scored with the stick inside this limited area.

HOCKEY CHRONOLOGY

1800s The modern game was started in England as an alternative to football for cricketers seeking a winter sport.

1861 First organised club was the Blackheath Football and Hockey Club.

1871 The birth of the Teddington Club and modern hockey.

1874 Richmond Football Club decided to try hockey as an offshoot of football.

1874 Surbiton Hockey Club is formed.

1886 Hockey Association (Men) is founded.

1886 Slazenger introduces a prototype of a spliced stick.

1895 All England Women's Hockey Association is founded becoming the first women's national sporting governing body.

1895 First men's international match is held. England beat Ireland 5-0.

1896 First women's international match. Ireland beat England 2-0.

1900 England has around 200 hockey clubs.

1908 Men's field hockey is first featured in the Olympic Games (held in London) with England, Ireland and Scotland competing separately.

1909 First steps towards an international federation when the Hockey Association in England and the Belgium Hockey Association agreed to mutually recognise each other to regulate international hockey. The French Association follows soon after.

1912 Hockey is dropped from the Stockholm Olympic Games.

1920s Clubs are set up in European countries such as Belgium, Denmark, France, Germany and Holland, with national associations being formed.

1920 Hockey is reinstated for the Antwerp Olympic Games.

1924 The International Hockey Federation, the world governing body for the sport, is founded in Paris under the initiative of Frenchman, Paul Leautey, who became the first president of the FIH.

1927 The Women's International Hockey Federation is formed.

1951 First women's international held at Wembley. England beat Ireland 6-1.

1958 First national domestic competition, the men's county championship is held.

1968 First national women's domestic competition is held.

1971 Men's World Cup is introduced.

1972 First national men's club competition is held, which was the forerunner to the men's cup competition.

1974 Seventy-one members are affiliated to the International Hockey Federation.

1980 Women's hockey is introduced to the Olympic Games.

1980s Both men's and women's national leagues are formed.

1980s Artificial grass pitches are introduced.

1981 Men's and women's International Hockey Federations join under the Fédération Internationale de Hockey (FIH).

1996 English Hockey Association is formed, to unite the separate governing bodies of men's, women's and mixed hockey, the first two of which had been in existence for over 100 years.

1997 Men's and women's national leagues come together as the English Hockey League.

2003 England Hockey formed.

2003 Reading men's team wins European Club Championships.

2003 Olton and West Warwickshire women win silver medal in European Club Championship.

2007 The Fédération Internationale de Hockey has 118 members.

2007 Australian Youth Olympic Festival in Australia; Great Britain girls win gold and the boys win silver.

INDEX

IMPERIAL/METRIC CONVERSION TABLE

Imperial	Metric	Imperial	Metric
100 yards	91.4 metres	5 feet	1.5 metres
60 yards	54.9 metres	4 feet	1.2 metres
55 yards	50.2 metres	18 inches	45.7 centimetres
50 yards	45.7 metres	9.25 inches	23.5 centimetres
40 yards	36.6 metres	9 inches	22.9 centimetres
25 yards	22.9 metres	8.81 inches	22.4 centimetres
16 yards	14.6 metres	6 inches	15.2 centimetres
10 yards	9.1 metres	3 inches	7.6 centimetres
7 yards	6.4 metres	2 inches	5.1 centimetres
5 yards	4.6 metres	28 ounces	794 grams
4 yards	3.6 metres	12 ounces	340 grams
1 yard	1 metre	5.75 ounces	163 grams
7 feet	2.1 metres	5.5 ounces	156 grams